Magnets in the Real World

by Chris Eboch

Content Consultant
Peter Barnes
Astrophysicist
University of Florida

CORE
LIBRARY

Published by ABDO Publishing Company, PO Box 398166, Minneapolis, MN 55439. Copyright © 2013 by Abdo Consulting Group, Inc. International copyrights reserved in all countries. No part of this book may be reproduced in any form without written permission from the publisher. The Core Library™ is a trademark and logo of ABDO Publishing Company.

Printed in the United States of America,
North Mankato, Minnesota
112012
012013

Editor: Karen Latchana Kenney
Series Designer: Becky Daum

Cataloging-in-Publication Data
Eboch, Chris.
 Magnets in the real world / Chris Eboch.
   p. cm. -- (Science in the real world)
Includes bibliographical references and index.
ISBN 978-1-61783-742-5
1. Magnetism--Juvenile literature.   I. Title.
538--dc21
                                        2012946802

Photo Credits: Lee Prince/Shutterstock Images, cover, 1; NOAA/Getty Images, 4; Shutterstock Images, 6, 8, 20, 25, 40; DEA/R.Appiani/De Agostini/Getty Images, 10; Universal Images Group/Getty Images, 12; SSPL/Getty Images, 15; Hulton Archive/Getty Images, 17; DK Images, 22; Red Line Editorial, 24, 30; Vladimir Gerasimov/Shutterstock Images, 27; NASA/AP Images, 28; Aleksandr Kurganov/Shutterstock Images, 31; Kurita KAKU/Gamma-Rapho/Getty Images, 34, 45; Elena Elisseeva/Shutterstock Images, 36; Dmitriy Shironosov/Shutterstock Images, 38

CONTENTS

CHAPTER ONE

The Power of Magnets

Magnets are in use all around us. Some are basic, and some are complex. Some are obvious, and others are hidden. But whether or not you see the magnet, powerful science is at work.

A magnet has the power to attract some objects. It can pull these objects closer as if on an invisible string. Magnets do not affect most objects. Magnets

Auroras are caused when solar winds blow space particles near Earth's magnetic field.

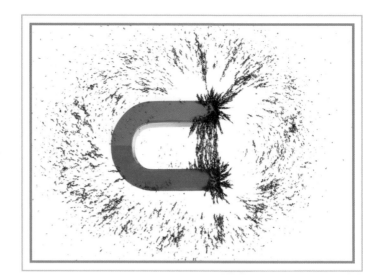

A magnet attracts iron filings toward its poles.

only work on some kinds of metal. They mainly attract iron, nickel, and cobalt. They attract steel objects, such as pins and needles. That's because steel contains iron. Something that is affected by a magnet has magnetic properties.

The power of magnets is called magnetic force. A magnet's force depends on how strong the magnet is and how far away it is from an object. A weak magnet may have to touch an object to pick it up. A very strong magnet may attract something from across the room. Magnetic force can even work through a barrier, such as cardboard.

Magnets All Around

Magnets are in many things we use every day. Some may hold papers on your refrigerator. The refrigerator also has a magnet around the edge of the door to hold the door closed. The refrigerator even has a magnet in its motor.

Magnets Make Magnets

One magnet can make another magnet. Some objects, such as iron nails and steel pins, can be turned into magnets. If you place a magnet on that object, the object will become magnetic too. But it may not be as strong as the first magnet.

You probably have many hidden magnets around your home. Televisions, video game consoles, and computers use magnets. Sound systems use magnets. Headphones have tiny magnets in them. Car engines use magnets too.

Many of these magnets are electromagnets. Electricity is used to turn the magnet on and off. This controls the magnet's power. These magnets are often

A compass uses a magnetic needle to show direction.

more powerful than most permanent magnets. Most machines use electromagnets.

The biggest magnet on Earth is Earth itself. The magnetic north and south poles attract other magnets. Long ago sailors and explorers realized they could use this power. They made compasses using magnetic needles. The needles were attracted to the poles, so they pointed north and south. Knowing those directions helped explorers find their way.

That was just the start of hundreds of inventions using magnets. Magnets continue to make our lives easier in many ways.

William Gilbert was an English doctor who studied magnets, which were once called lodestones (spelled loadstones in this passage). In 1600 he wrote a book called *On the Loadstone and Magnetic Bodies and on the Great Magnet the Earth*. He said:

> [T]he loadstone has from nature its two poles, a northern and a southern . . . [These poles are] fixed, definite points in the stone. . . . These poles look toward the poles of the earth, and move toward them, and are subject to them. The magnetic poles may be found in every loadstone, whether strong and powerful . . . or faint [and] weak. . . . [This is true] whether it be long, or flat, or four-square, or three-cornered or polished; whether it be rough, broken-off, or unpolished: the loadstone ever has and ever shows its poles.

Source: William Gilbert. On the Loadstone and Magnetic Bodies and on the Great Magnet the Earth. *Translated by P. Fleury Mottelay. London: Bernard Quaritch, 1893. Print. 23.*

Back It Up

Read Gilbert's quote carefully. What point is he trying to make? How is this idea supported by details? Name two supporting details.

CHAPTER TWO

The Secrets of Magnets

Ancient people discovered that a rare rock had magnetic properties. They saw that it could attract iron. They called this type of rock *lodestone*. The Greeks wrote about lodestone around 600 BCE. Great Greek thinkers studied magnetism, but they could not figure out how it worked.

The Chinese also used lodestones. They discovered that they could create a new magnet by

We now know that lodestone is the naturally magnetized mineral magnetite.

William Gilbert was interested in magnets and Earth's magnetic field.

rubbing a steel needle on a lodestone. They placed

this needle in a tiny floating boat in a bowl of water.

The magnet always pointed in a fixed direction. It was

a crude compass. Travelers could tell direction even

if they were far out at sea with this compass. These

compasses were first described in writing in 1086 CE.

Arabs and Europeans soon learned about compasses. By 1580 many travelers were using them. The compass helped people make great voyages across the sea. With the help of the compass, Christopher Columbus found the way from Spain to America. Other great explorers also used compasses as they explored the world.

Understanding Magnets

People used compasses, but they did not understand them. Why did lodestone have special qualities? How could lodestone turn needles magnetic? What was this force that pulled magnets in a certain direction?

The First Magnets

The first magnets were natural. Some rocks may have become magnets when Earth first cooled. Others may have been hit by lightning, which carries a very strong electric current.

Some scientists experimented. They hoped to understand magnets. William Gilbert was a doctor in England. He spent a lot of time studying magnetism. Gilbert believed Earth was a giant magnet. He ran experiments to check his idea. The results of his experiments confirmed his theory. In 1600 he published a book to share his findings with the world. The book was called *De Magnete*, which means "on the magnet."

This was a big step forward in understanding magnetism. Still scientists had much more to learn. They knew some things about magnets. They knew some things about electricity. But they did not yet realize how the two forces were connected.

Many scientists studied electricity in the early 1800s. One was a Danish professor named Hans Christian Ørsted. In 1820 he held a scientific demonstration. He showed his friends how he could heat a wire with an electric current. He also had a compass nearby for a show of magnetism. He noticed

Fig. 9.

Hans Christian Oerfted.

that when he connected the wire to a current, the compass needle moved. He did not understand why, but he wrote an article about what he saw. He had made a simple electromagnet, but he didn't realize it.

Other scientists tried the same experiment and got the same results. André-Marie Ampère in France was one of these scientists. Also in 1820, he realized magnetism was the force between electric currents. Magnetism and electricity were connected.

Electricity and Magnetism

Michael Faraday was an English scientist. He studied magnets and electricity and showed how the two could be used together. In 1831 he tried some experiments to make a magnet with electricity. He sent an electric current through a wire wound around an iron ring. The electricity made the iron ring magnetic. That made another piece of wire on the other side of the ring magnetic. Faraday could turn the magnetism on and off. How? He only had to turn the electricity on and off. This was a simple electromagnet.

In the United States, Joseph Henry made improvements to Faraday's electromagnet. In 1832 Henry built an electromagnet. It could lift 3,600 pounds (1,600 kg). That's as much as the weight of a car.

Michael Faraday experimented with an iron ring and electricity to make a magnet.

17

Static Electricity

Electricity sometimes attracts things the way magnets do. Static electricity can cause clothes to cling to each other when they come out of the dryer. It can cause long hair to stick out from a person's head in dry weather. Static electricity has to do with the behavior of electrons, just like with magnets. Magnets and electricity sometimes act alike, but they don't work on the same objects.

With the help of electromagnets, people can build powerful machines. Electromagnets are used in cars, fast trains, and scientific equipment. Small versions are used in many things you may have at home.

Michael Faraday kept journals and wrote letters and articles. In 1831 he wrote about his recent research in a letter:

> *I am busy just now again on Electro-Magnetism and think I have got hold of a good thing but can't say; it may be a weed instead of a fish that after all my labour I may at last pull up. I think I know why metals are magnetic when in motion though not (generally) when at rest.*

Source: Michael Faraday. The Life and Letters of Faraday, Volume 2. Bence Jones, ed. London: Longmans, Green, and Co., 1870. Print. 3.

Consider Your Audience

Review Faraday's quote closely. Consider how you would adapt it for a different audience, such as your parents, your principal, or younger friends. Write a blog post conveying this same information for the new audience. Write it so that it can be understood by them. What is the most effective way to get your point across to this audience? How does your new approach differ from the original text, and why?

CHAPTER THREE

Magnetism at Work

To understand magnetism, you have to understand electrons. They are smaller than anything you can see. You and everything around you are made up of molecules. For example, a drop of water is made up of many trillions of water molecules. Molecules are made up of smaller parts called atoms. A single atom is so small that it is

Many atoms and electrons are in a single drop of water.

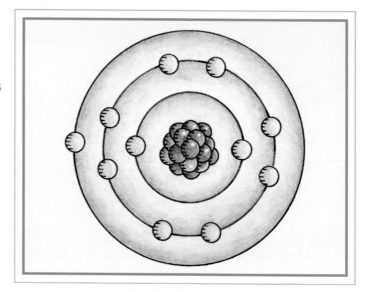

Electrons (shown as yellow) move around the nucleus of an atom, which contains protons (shown as red) and neutrons (shown as green).

invisible. But an atom is made up of even smaller particles, including electrons.

Atoms and Electrons

At the center of an atom is its nucleus. Protons and neutrons are inside the nucleus. Electrons spin around an atom's nucleus. As they do, they create very tiny magnetic fields. A magnetic field acts like a magnet. Every electron has this tiny magnetic field. In most materials, electrons pair up. The paired electrons spin in different directions. The magnetic field of one electron cancels out the magnetic field of another. That means the material as a whole is not a magnet.

In some materials, such as iron, the electrons do not form pairs. They can spin freely and line up in the same direction. Small groups of atoms then cluster together. They form small magnetic areas called domains. Each domain has trillions of atoms in it. Magnetic domains are usually a few millimeters in size.

In each domain, all the electrons' magnetic fields line up. Still the iron is not magnetic. The different domains are not lined up with each other. Since they are not aligned, they cancel each other out.

That changes if you put a piece of iron into a magnetic field. All the domains line up and start to point in the same direction. The piece of iron then becomes a permanent magnet. It will remain a magnet unless something happens to stop it from being a magnet.

Opposite Poles

When the domains point in one direction, a magnet's force has direction. Every magnet has a north pole and a south pole. The magnetic force is strongest at

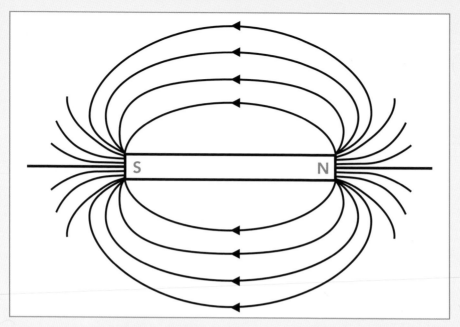

Magnetic Field Lines
This diagram shows magnetic field lines around a magnet.
How does this diagram relate to what you read in the text?
Does it help you understand how a magnet works?

these poles. The magnetic field spreads out from the north pole. It then circles back to the south pole and enters the magnet again. The field lines form a loop, going out, around, and back in.

Identifying a magnet's poles is easiest if the magnet is a bar shape. Magnets can also come in other shapes, such as squares, rings, and horseshoes. A magnet's shape can make it harder to identify the poles, but the poles are still there. If you cut a

A horseshoe magnet's poles are clearly marked.

magnet into pieces, each piece will still have north and south poles.

Magnets pull toward each other in some positions and push away in others. With two magnets, their opposite poles are attracted. One magnet's north pole is pulled to the other magnet's south pole. Poles that are the same repel. One magnet's north pole pushes away from the other magnet's north pole. The south poles push away from each other too.

Magnetic Fields

Magnetic fields are invisible, but they have visible effects. You can use iron filings to see the shape or effects of a magnetic field. Sprinkle the iron filings on top of a piece of paper, and then set the paper on top of a magnet. The iron filings will move into the magnetic field lines. Some toys use magnets. One toy lets the user move iron filings into the hair or a beard on a picture of a man.

Magnets can exert their force through some barriers. If the barrier is thick, a weak magnet won't work. And the magnet's power can be affected by what the barrier is made of. A magnet will stick to a steel plate, but it can't move something on the other side.

Magnetic Tricks

Magicians use magnets for some tricks. They might hold a magnet under a table, where it's hidden. As they slide the magnet around, it moves an object on top of the table. The object looks like it's moving on its own.

Magnets hold darts to a magnetic dartboard.

CHAPTER FOUR

The Earth as a Magnet

Magnets come in many shapes and sizes. The biggest magnet on Earth is Earth itself. Earth's magnetic field is produced at its center. Earth's inner core is a solid iron ball about as hot as the surface of the sun. Around the inner core is the outer core. This is a deep layer of liquid iron, similar to an ocean floating around the inner core.

Earth is one giant magnet.

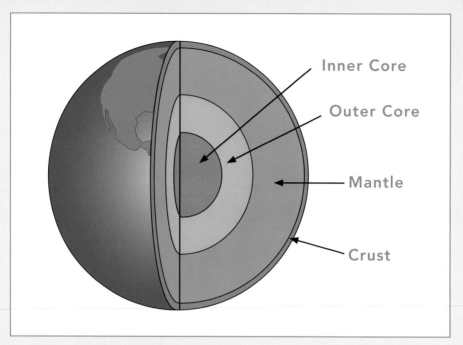

Inside Earth's Core
This is a diagram of Earth's core. How does this diagram
compare to the information at the beginning of the chapter?
Can you use that information to explain what makes up the
inner core and outer core?

This outer core creates Earth's magnetic field, because

iron has magnetic properties.

No one has been to Earth's core. Scientists

make predictions based on what they see on Earth's

surface. They also study earthquake waves that travel

through Earth. They use math and computer models

to test their ideas. The magnetic properties of Earth

The rod through this model of Earth shows where the geographic poles are located.

are not perfectly understood. Scientists are still studying them.

Magnetic versus Geographic

Just like a small magnet, Earth has north and south poles. In magnetic terms, these poles are where the magnetic field enters and leaves Earth. However, people use the terms *north pole* and *south pole* in several different ways.

The geographic poles are the most southern and northern points on Earth's surface. These are the points where Earth rotates on its axis. Earth spins like a giant top, with the north pole at the top and the south pole at the bottom. The north pole is in the middle of the frozen Arctic Ocean. The south pole is on the continent of Antarctica.

The geographic poles are different from the magnetic poles. The magnetic north pole is currently located off the coast of Greenland. This is where the magnetic field enters Earth. The north end of a compass points to this pole. The magnetic south pole is where Earth's magnetic field points directly away from Earth. The magnetic south pole is currently in Antarctica.

Animal Magnets

Many animals migrate, or move from one region to another, every year. Some may get help from Earth's magnetic field. Some animals have a magnetic mineral in their bodies. This might act as a compass. Whales, dolphins, turtles, birds, and butterflies are thought to use Earth's magnetic field when they migrate.

The south end of the compass points to this spot. When you are at a magnetic pole, the magnetic field is straight up or straight down. A compass is then useless.

The magnetic poles don't stay in one place. They are constantly changing. Scientists keep track of the magnetic poles as they change. In recent years, the magnetic north pole has been moving north to northwest.

CHAPTER FIVE

Magnets in Our World

Magnets vary a lot in strength. A refrigerator magnet is strong enough to hold up a piece of paper. The most powerful permanent magnet is much stronger. Powerful permanent magnets have a lot of metal in them. That makes them large and heavy. To get the most out of magnets, we need ones that are small and strong.

Powerful magnets are used in a maglev train in Japan.

A plug connects a wire to a current through an outlet.

On-and-Off Magnets

A magnetic field that moves or changes can create an electric current. This is known as electromagnetic induction. Electromagnets are not permanent, but they have a big advantage. They can be far stronger than permanent magnets.

The simplest electromagnet is a wire connected to a current. This creates a magnetic field. The field can be turned on or off as the current is turned on or off. Usually this magnetic field isn't very powerful. The wires attached to your household appliances all have magnetic fields. However, they are not noticeable.

Coiling the wire in a circle creates a stronger magnetic field. Coiling it into many loops makes the magnetic field even more powerful. Coils are used to create strong magnets for many uses.

Magnets in the Home

Several common home devices use magnets. Microwave ovens produce electromagnetic waves. These waves cause water molecules to move around and rub each other. This friction heats the water in food or drinks. The electromagnetic waves only heat water. That means the microwave oven itself does not get hot inside.

Computers use magnets as well. A computer hard drive has disks coated with a magnetic metal. Over the years, researchers have found ways to improve computer hard drives and disks. They have made

Computers contain magnets.

them smaller and more powerful. Now this technology is used in other devices, such as MP3 players and video games.

Start Your Engines

Electromagnets are also useful because they can be turned on and off. Most cars today run on gasoline burned in an engine. To start that engine, a spark is needed to ignite the fuel. This starts with the ignition coils. A battery produces a surge of electric current. This makes a magnetic field in the coils. It increases the power from the battery. The coils then produce a spark. The spark ignites the fuel and starts the engine.

Maglev trains use magnets in order to move. These trains have electromagnets on board. The whole train rides in a magnetic field above iron rails. The train does not even need wheels, because it floats just above the surface. These trains can travel very quickly and quietly.

Magnets in Medicine

Magnetic resonance imaging (MRI) machines are used to find problems in our bodies. Human bodies have a slight reaction to magnetic fields. An MRI machine sends pulses into the

Electric Guitars

Electric guitars use electricity and magnetism to make the sound louder. The guitar strings vibrate when plucked. This creates the music, but it is very quiet. A magnetic part called the pickup turns vibrations into electric signals. The signals are then sent to an amplifier and speaker.

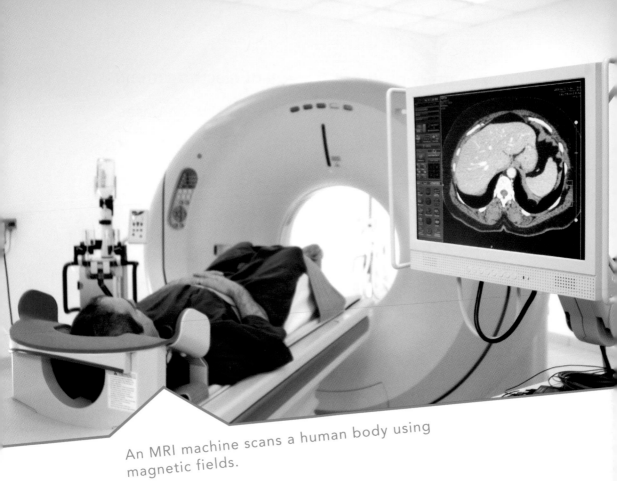

An MRI machine scans a human body using magnetic fields.

body. Depending on what is in an area, a different signal is sent back. These different signals show different types of bone and tissue.

Magnets are everywhere. They help us keep our food cold and heat it up. Magnets are used in computers and video games. They allow people to travel quickly from place to place on maglev trains

and in cars. Magnets are in machines large and small.
And the largest magnet is beneath our feet—Earth.
Life would not be the same without magnets in
our world.

EXPLORE ONLINE

The focus in Chapter Five was the many ways magnets
are used. It also touched upon MRIs. The Web site below
focuses on MRIs. As you know, every source is different.
How is the information given in the Web site different
from the information in this chapter? What information is
the same? How do the two sources present information
differently? What can you learn from this Web site?

Magnetic Resonance Imaging
www.kidshealth.org/parent/system/medical/mri.html

IMPORTANT DATES

600s BCE
Ancient Greeks write about lodestone.

1086 CE
The Chinese describe compasses in writing.

1580
Many travelers use compasses to make voyages across the sea.

1600
William Gilbert publishes a book stating that Earth is a giant magnet.

1820
Hans Christian Ørsted accidentally discovers that electric current affects magnetism.

1820
André-Marie Ampère in France realizes magnetism is the force between electric currents.

1831
Michael Faraday creates a simple electromagnet.

1832
Joseph Henry builds an electromagnet that can lift 3,600 pounds (1,600 kg).

OTHER WAYS YOU CAN FIND MAGNETS IN THE REAL WORLD

Computers

Computers can hold large amounts of information. Hard drives use disks called platters to store that information. These disks are made of magnetic material. An electromagnet writes on the disk. It magnetizes small sections in different directions. The directions stand for ones and zeros. Patterns of ones and zeros can be read as words, numbers, or symbols.

Recycling

Many recycling centers use magnets to separate items. This works best to pull out iron and steel. Simple magnetism does not work on other metals. It can also have trouble with objects made from a mixture of metals. Other metals can be pulled out of garbage if they conduct electricity. This kind of separator uses forces that make objects repel. Materials jump off a conveyor belt away from the force. This works well on aluminum objects, such as soda pop cans.

Metal Detectors

Metal detectors use electromagnetic induction to identify metal. A pulsing electric current creates a magnetic field. When that moves across metal, the magnetic field creates electric currents. Those electric currents create another magnetic field. This signals the presence of metal.

STOP AND THINK

Say What?

Studying magnets can mean learning a lot of new vocabulary. Find five words in this book you have never seen or heard before. Find out what they mean. Then write the meanings in your own words, and use each word in a new sentence.

Another View

There are many sources online and in your library about magnets. Ask a librarian or other adult to help you find a reliable source on magnets. Compare what you learn in this new source and what you have found out in this book. Then write a short essay comparing and contrasting the new source's view of magnets to the ideas in this book. How are they different? How are they similar? Why do you think they are different or similar?

Tell the Tale

This book discusses how people learned about the forces of magnetism. Write 200 words that tell the true story of the history of our understanding of magnetism. Be sure to set the scene, develop a sequence of events, and offer a conclusion.

Surprise Me

The history and study of magnets can be interesting and surprising. What two or three facts about magnets did you find most surprising? Write a few sentences about each fact. Why did you find them surprising?

GLOSSARY

current
the movement of electricity through a wire

force
an action that changes the shape or movement of an object

domain
a small region of a substance that is magnetic

induction
producing an electrical or magnetic effect

electromagnet
a temporary magnet formed when electricity flows through a coil of wire

migrate
to move away from one area at a certain time of year to live in a different climate

electron
a tiny particle that moves around the nucleus of an atom

nucleus
the central part of an atom that is made of neutrons and protons

LEARN MORE

Books

Angliss, Sarah, and Maggie Hewson. *Hands-On Science: Electricity and Magnets.* New York: Kingfisher, 2013.

McGregor, Harriet. *Magnets and Springs.* New York: Windmill Books, 2011.

Sandner, Lionel. *What is Electromagnetism?* New York: Crabtree, 2012.

Web Links

To learn more about magnets, visit ABDO Publishing Company online at **www.abdopublishing.com**. Web sites about magnets are featured on our Book Links page. These links are routinely monitored and updated to provide the most current information available.

Visit **www.mycorelibrary.com** for free additional tools for teachers and students.

INDEX

ABOUT THE AUTHOR

Chris Eboch writes about science, history, and culture for all ages. Her novels for young people include historical fiction, ghost stories, and action-packed adventures.